Grieving the Loss of Your Child

Comfort for Your Broken Heart

Ryan Showalter

New Growth Press

www.newgrowthpress.com

New Growth Press, Greensboro, NC 27404
www.newgrowthpress.com
Copyright © 2014 by Ryan Showalter

Cover Design: Faceout Books, faceoutstudio.com
Typesetting: Lisa Parnell, Thompson's Station, TN

ISBN: 978-1-939946-92-8 (Print)
ISBN: 978-1-939946-93-5 (eBook)

Library of Congress Cataloging-in-Publication Data
Showalter, Ryan, 1985–
  Grieving the loss of your child : comfort for your broken heart
/ Ryan Showalter.
     pages cm
  ISBN 978-1-939946-92-8 — ISBN 978-1-939946-93-5
(ebook) 1. Children—Death—Religious aspects—
Christianity. 2. Grief—Religious aspects—Christianity.
3. Bereavement—Religious aspects—Christianity. I. Title.
  BV4907.S47 2014
  248.8'66—dc23
                                                    2014026238
Printed in Canada

21 20 19 18 17 16 15 14   1 2 3 4 5

John and Julie were eagerly expecting their first child after struggling many months to get pregnant. They were excited at the prospect of being parents for the first time, but given the medical issues surrounding their trouble conceiving, they were also worried about the baby. The first signs of concern came just thirteen weeks into the pregnancy. At twenty-two weeks, Julie delivered a stillborn baby boy.

Instead of welcoming him into their home, they were tragically confronted with the task of saying goodbye at the cemetery. Faced with an enemy they never expected, death robbed them of the joys and struggles of raising their firstborn son.

My brother David was two years old. I was nine and relatively oblivious to the brokenness of the world. Our family lived in a quiet, old suburban neighborhood where we freely roamed with friends and only came home for meals. Our ignorance of the world's harshness changed in an instant on a crisp fall afternoon. While playing with the big kids in our family's front yard, David was struck and killed by a runaway car. Death literally came to our doorstep, and we were suddenly confronted with an enemy we were unprepared to face.

The Bible identifies death as an enemy, and the death of your child is the worst kind of enemy. It ruthlessly wreaks havoc on the way things should be and leaves devastation and heartache in its wake. I am so sorry—sorry that your beautiful child is gone; sorry that your world has crashed down around you; sorry that life will never again feel normal, that things are no longer the way they should be. I am sorry for the weight of grief that threatens to crush you at a moment's notice.

I am so sorry, but I am not without hope for you and your family—hope that you will find comfort in the shelter of the Almighty (Psalm 91:1). Hope that God will give you the help you need exactly when you need it; hope that you can be honest with God and experience his presence with you in your suffering; hope that the One who defeated death will keep the death of your child from defeating you.

My desire is that this minibook will help you in two ways: First, that you will be connected to the comfort, hope, and help that God alone provides. Second, that it will offer practical wisdom for drawing on those resources in the shadow of your child's death. Everyday undertakings often seem impossible in light of grief, and you are to be commended for cracking the cover of this minibook. May God use it to connect you to his mercy and grace in the days ahead.

God Is Not Far Off

Grief is your unique response to the loss of your child. It is, according to Jay Adams, "a life-shaking sorrow."[1] Accordingly, it should not be viewed as a simple emotion, but as a reaction within which a range of emotions will be present. Grief often acts as a barrier between you and the world, isolating you from the people and circumstances of everyday life. Foods lose their taste, colors seem to fade, and the most mundane tasks become insurmountable obstacles. Most troubling of all, God may seem distant and removed, as if he is not with you in the midst of your new reality, one you never imagined would be yours.

The psalmist records the prayer of an afflicted man, desperately crying out to God in his hardship.

> For my days vanish like smoke;
>   my bones burn like glowing embers.
> My heart is blighted and withered like grass;
>   I forget to eat my food.
> In my distress I groan aloud
>   and am reduced to skin and bones.
> (Psalm 102:3–5)

As you mourn the loss of your child, you may identify with these words from the psalmist, wondering if God will hear your cry and comfort you in your suffering. You may feel as if your heart has withered and that you are no longer able to love, think, or relate as you did in the past. The Scriptures accurately describe the honest emotions of a grieving heart because God understands your pain and your grief. Thankfully, God does not leave you alone in your grief. The Scriptures also portray God as one who actively responds to the suffering of his people.

Where is God in your suffering? God is not far off from the afflicted. He has not distanced himself from you or your suffering. He cares deeply about you as you struggle in the midst of your grief. The psalmist recognizes God's faithfulness even in the midst of great anguish: "The LORD is close to the brokenhearted and saves those who are crushed in spirit" (Psalm 34:18). God does not move away from you as you suffer; indeed, the Scripture promises that he "is near to all who call on him" (Psalm 145:18), especially when you call on him in the midst of the toughest circumstances imaginable.

The temptation to doubt God's presence and love in the wake of tragedy is strong. You may be wondering if God has forgotten you or if his love for you has failed in some way. In fact, nothing could be further from the truth. The Bible characterizes Jesus, the Son of God and second member of the Trinity, as a despised and rejected man of sorrows who is familiar with grief (Isaiah 53:3).

Just when God seems most distant and unloving, Scripture reminds us that Jesus was "overwhelmed with sorrow to the point of death" before his arrest, trial, and crucifixion (Matthew 26:38). He asked his disciples to keep watch with him as he prayed, but they abandoned him to catch some sleep instead. However, Jesus is not like his disciples. He will not abandon you when you are overwhelmed with sorrow to the point of despair. Jesus, who knows what it is to be abandoned in the face of suffering, will never leave you alone.

Rather than leaving us to suffer in solitude, God comes to meet us. Jesus entered into creation and experienced suffering just like you and me so that we would never suffer alone. We now have the opportunity to approach God with confidence because we know he is not distant and aloof. Instead Jesus knows exactly what we are going through because he voluntarily went through the same trials, temptations, sufferings, and worse. Jesus, by entering into our world and our suffering, is uniquely qualified to offer help and hope when we need it most. Therefore, rather than grieving alone, in Christ we "receive mercy and find grace to help us in our time of need" (Hebrews 4:16).

God is near to you, grieving father; God is near to you, grieving mother. He stubbornly refuses to abandon you to your pain, and instead offers mercy, grace, and the comforting presence of One who also lost a child. Though in your suffering he may seem far off, Scripture reminds us that he has drawn near to you precisely because of your suffering. His love and concern for you cannot be overcome. Just as he was faithful to meet the needs of his people in their desert wanderings, he will meet your needs now, even as you trek through the barren desert of grief and suffering.

You Can Be Honest with God

One temptation that may threaten to ensnare you as you mourn the death of your child is what I call the "doing well" temptation. When family, friends, or acquaintances ask how you are doing, you reply with a forced "I'm good," or "We're doing well," or "We're managing alright," though nothing could be further from the truth. We are trained to do this throughout our lives—giving inauthentic answers to inauthentic questions, neither party really wanting to dig deep and share in the realities of life in a broken world. In the midst of your grief it may seem the easier, less-messy path to give a rote answer when asked how you are doing, and at times it may indeed be appropriate. The danger in this, however, comes when you begin to address God, your Creator and King, with the same arm's-length transactions you do inquiring friends.

The writer of Psalm 77 was in the midst of a desperate situation. He recounts crying out to

God for help, being distressed, and being too troubled even to speak. In his desperation, he wonders

> "Will the Lord reject forever?
>> Will he never show his favor again?
> Has his unfailing love vanished forever?
>> Has his promise failed for all time?
> Has God forgotten to be merciful?
>> Has he in anger withheld his
>>> compassion?"
> (Psalm 77:7–9)

These brutally honest questions are not met with condemnation from God. God did not express exasperation that one of his people came to him in the middle of a troubled time with heavy questions that defied pat answers. God is not like a friend who struggles to handle your honest emotion. He is not like a casual acquaintance you might fear putting in an awkward situation if you really open up about the state of your well-being. God created the heavens and the earth and sustains them moment-by-moment. In fact, the book of Colossians reminds us that in Jesus, all things hold together (Colossians 1:17). So God was not overwhelmed by the honesty of the psalmist, and he will not be overwhelmed by your honesty either.

In an article on Psalm 77, Pat Graham writes that the psalmist "rejects superficial, inadequate attempts at consolation. His questionings are deep and earnest, because his faith itself has been challenged."[2] Perhaps your faith has been challenged by the death of your child as well. You need not hide that fact or feel ashamed about it; the Scriptures testify that the very same thing happened with the psalmist.

Where can you turn when your faith is challenged? When, as Michael Milton puts it, "the definition of God and our expectations of him clash with a life-shaking reality," to whom do you go for comfort and help?[3] Here again we refer to the psalmist and can learn from his experience:

> Then I thought, "To this I will appeal:
>   the years when the Most High stretched
>   out his right hand."
> I will remember the deeds of the Lord;
>   yes, I will remember your miracles of
>   long ago.
> I will consider all your works
>   and meditate on all your mighty deeds.
> Your ways, God, are holy.
>   What god is as great as our God?
> You are the God who performs miracles;
>   you display your power among the
>   peoples.

With your mighty arm you redeemed
    your people,
  the descendants of Jacob and Joseph.
(Psalm 77:10–15)

Rather than being taken aback or put off by the psalmist's honest cries for help, God reminds the psalmist of his enduring love and faithfulness. God's message of comfort and reassurance to the psalmist is essentially this: "No matter how bad things get in the world, I have not left my people alone."

That message is for you as well. Come to God with your broken heart. Come to him with your pain and anguish. Come to him with your honest questions. Come to him with your shaken faith. He has good news for you, even now, even when you are hurting most. He has comfort for you, even now, when you are inconsolable and over-whelmed with grief.

What is this good news? What is this comfort? It is this: things in this world are badly broken, but they will not always be so, and until all things are restored to their right function, God will never leave you or forsake you. This was his reminder to the psalmist, and it is his reminder to you too. God is active. He is on the move. His kingdom is coming—a kingdom where death is defeated, its effects erased, and every tear is wiped from every eye.

Your Father in heaven longs to hear from you. He knows your pain, so bring it to him honestly. No fronts, no appearances. In his kingdom there is no question too difficult or emotion too raw. Remember that Jesus suffered, died, and was resurrected to secure for you a certain approach to God's throne of grace. This is God's sovereign plan to ensure that in Christ you will receive mercy and find grace to help you in your time of need.

Grieving with Hope

The apostle Paul, in his first letter to the Thessalonian church, cautioned the believers against grieving "like the rest of mankind, who have no hope" (1 Thessalonians 4:13). But what does it mean to grieve with hope? Is that really possible after the death of your child? *Hope* may be the one emotion you feel sure you'll never experience again, the one thing that will always be just beyond your grasp. Is Paul's message to the Thessalonians a pie-in-the-sky dream of one who never experienced the depths of grief, or is it a helpful, practical, and grace-filled reminder that life lived in the kingdom of God is fundamentally different than life lived any other way?

God's message to you, delivered through Paul, is decidedly not pie-in-the-sky. How can we be sure? If anyone would reject a fanciful message about grief, it would have been Paul, the shipwrecked, stoned, and persecuted apostle. During his battle with a tormenting messenger of Satan, Paul pleaded for God to remove the cause of his suffering. Instead, God taught Paul that it is in human weakness that he is able to work most effectively. God's grace was sufficient for Paul, and it will prove sufficient for you as well. Just as Paul learned to grieve with hope, so can you. Here are four practical strategies that will equip you to grieve with hope:

1) Draw Near to God

According to the Scriptures, "the eyes of the LORD range throughout the earth to strengthen those whose hearts are fully committed to him" (2 Chronicles 16:9). The commitment this verse speaks of is a humble reliance on the Lord in times of trouble, not a mustering of human performance to prove oneself worthy before God. Even now, bereaved parent, you can express full commitment to the Lord by calling on him in your distress and seeing that he will answer (Psalm 120:1). Paul's discovery that weakness leads to strength in the kingdom of God is good news for you. In your grief-induced weakness, you can be made strong by the power of God if you will call on him.

Remember, your ability to carry on with spiritual disciplines, such as reading your Bible and prayer, are not the basis of your fellowship with

God. Church attendance and ministry involvement are not the basis of your fellowship with God. Jesus has secured your standing with God, so no matter how distant or unspiritual you may feel in the wake of your child's death, God will not turn his back on you. In fact, if you are in Christ, he cannot turn his back on you because "Christ also suffered once for sins, the righteous for the unrighteous, to bring you to God" (1 Peter 3:18). You cannot undo with your weakened faith what Christ has completed in his death and resurrection.

Take hope in that glorious reality! In the kingdom of God, your weakness is actually your strength. Draw near to God, and he will draw near to you. He will never leave you. He will never forsake you. Practice fellowship with him by calling out to him, and he will answer you. Grief often comes in waves. Sometimes you are unexpectedly overcome with what happened. When you feel like you are drowning in a wave of grief, call out to Jesus for mercy and help. He will help you. It is in his gracious answers and faithful presence that you will find reason to grieve with hope.

2) Draw Near to Your Immediate Family

In times of grief, there is a temptation to draw inward. After all, your experience in grief is unique, so who could possibly understand what you are going through? Even your spouse, the one with whom you share life most intimately, may seem to be on a totally different page. Your parents, siblings, and other children may never understand exactly what you are feeling, but God has given them to you as a good gift, and you will need them in the days ahead.

Author Nancy Guthrie compares "the effect of grief on marriage to a train going over a wooden bridge."[4] If the bridge is already weak, the weight of the train may cause it to collapse; however, even if the bridge is strong, the weight of the train will still reveal stressed areas that require attention.[5] Drawing near to your spouse in the dark days after your child's death may be difficult. In fact, it may seem impossible. The pull of grief to focus inward is strong, but the all-sufficient grace of your God is even stronger. God has united you and your spouse together as one flesh, and though you will each grieve uniquely, you remain one nevertheless.

Resist also the temptation to measure your grief against that of your family. Remember that grief is a response characterized by varied emotions. On a day when you feel as if the world is crashing down around you, your spouse may want to talk about fond memories of your child. You are both grieving, but in drastically different ways; neither is better than the other. Neither response demonstrates more care or longing for your child. James's letter to the church teaches us to be "quick to listen, slow to speak and slow to become angry" (James 1:19). Seek to extend grace to one another and listen with compassion, just as your Father in heaven does for you.

Take small steps to remain connected to your spouse and family. Intentionally converse, pray, and share memories of your child to build unity in your family when isolation threatens to take hold. When you need a break from people (and you will; that's alright), retreat not into solitude but into the shelter of the Most High, and receive his mercy and grace. Remaining connected to your family, and especially your spouse, will help you grieve with hope in the days ahead.

3) Draw Near to God's People

The people of God have a very specific ministry to those who are grieving. Paul instructs the believers in Romans 12:15 to mourn with those who mourn. In his letter to the Corinthians, he tells them to "comfort those in any trouble with the comfort we ourselves receive from God" (2 Corinthians 1:4). Not only does God refuse to turn away from you, he has also arranged for people to come alongside and help you in your time of need. Everyday tasks such as grocery shopping, food preparation, and lawn care sometimes seem like burdens too heavy to bear in the shadow of grief, and that is normal. God knew your need ahead of time and prepared a group of people to help you.

If you are connected to a local church, let them know how they can help. You are not a burden to them; you are one in need of comfort, and they can help provide that comfort by meeting practical needs as they arise.

If you are not connected to a local church, ask the person who gave you this minibook to help you get connected. If members of a local church have hurt you before and you feel burned by the church, I am sorry. God's people are not perfect, but they have been called and equipped to minister to you in this time of need. They are part of God's plan for you in this troubled time. Let them mourn with you, let them comfort you, and let them encourage hopefulness in the midst of your grief.

4) Prepare Your Heart to Forgive

If the death of your child was caused by the negligence or sin of another, I am so very sorry. According to Robert Jones, "an offense that cuts deeply or turns our world upside down" is likely to lead to bitterness.[6] Someone's sin or negligence contributing to the death of your child is certainly such an offense. Bitterness is an attitude that sets the offended one against the perpetrator in judgment. Paul says in Ephesians, "Get rid of all bitterness, rage and anger, brawling and slander, along with every form of malice" (Ephesians 4:31).

How can you resist the temptation to adopt an attitude of bitterness toward the one whose actions caused your heart-wrenching loss? It will certainly not happen by accepting a shallow apology or attempting to shrug off the offense. Instead, Scripture points you to a better way. Paul continues in Ephesians 4:32, saying that Christians are to be "kind and compassionate to one another, forgiving each other, just as in Christ God forgave you." An attitude of forgiveness before God and granting forgiveness toward the offender are the two components of biblical forgiveness.

Through the death and resurrection of Jesus, the debt you owe God for your sin has been paid in full, at absolutely no cost to you. When you recognize that truth, you will be motivated to adopt an attitude of forgiveness rather than bitterness toward your offender. It certainly will not feel easy and it may take time, but the biblical correlation between being forgiven by God and being willing to forgive others is clear.

You will need help to be able to do this, and Jesus shows us where to find it in the prayer he taught his disciples: "forgive us our debts, as we also have forgiven our debtors" (Matthew 6:12). When you ask God to forgive your sins, ask him also to help you forgive. Once you have adopted an attitude of forgiveness before God, you can also have an attitude of forgiveness toward those who have hurt you. By God's grace and over time, you will even be able to forgive the one whose actions caused the death of your child when he or she confesses the sin to you and asks for forgiveness.[7]

When you forgive, you are promising to lay down the gavel of judgment and the sword of punishment, for those belong to God alone. You are not committing to forget the offense, which is impossible. Rather, you are committing to willfully restrain yourself from letting it stand between you and the offender, just as God has done for you in Christ. These are difficult promises, yes, but since God has extended them to you as one who caused the death of his Son, you can extend them to another—even one who caused the death of your child. As you extend the hope of God's forgiveness to a fellow sinner in need, you will be able to find hopefulness in your grief because you have resisted the temptation to become mired in bitterness.

Conclusion

The words of Psalm 23 depict a shepherd lovingly leading his sheep through the darkest valleys of life. He leads them to green pastures and quiet waters, and when trouble comes, he restores their souls. The constant presence of the shepherd in the midst of incredible hardship is the basis for David's assurance that "goodness and love will follow me all the days of my life, and I will dwell in the house of the LORD forever" (Psalm 23:6).

You also are not left alone in your grief. Though your world has been shattered by the death of your child, Jesus the good shepherd has laid down his life for you and will not abandon you when the wolves of pain and despair are circling. God is with you; God is for you; and God has mercy and grace for you through Jesus. When the pain of your child's death overwhelms you, may God lead you beside quiet waters and restore your soul.

Endnotes

1. Jay E. Adams, "Grief Counseling as an Opportunity" in *The Big Umbrella . . . and Other Essays and Addresses on Christian Counseling* (Grand Rapids: Baker Book House, 1972), 66.

2. Pat Graham, "Psalm 77: A Study in Faith and History," *Restoration Quarterly* 18, no. 3 (1975): 151–58, http://faculty.gordon.edu/hu/bi/ted_hildebrandt/otesources/19-psalms/text/articles/graham-ps77-rq.pdf. (accessed April 10, 2014).

3. Michael A. Milton, *Songs in the Night: How God Transforms Our Pain to Praise* (Phillipsburg, NJ: P&R Publishing, 2011), 2.

4. David and Nancy Guthrie, *When Your Family's Lost a Loved One: Finding Hope Together* (Carol Stream, IL: Tyndale House Publishers, 2008), 4.

5. Ibid.

6. Robert D. Jones, *Freedom from Resentment: Stopping Hurts from Turning Bitter* (Greensboro: New Growth Press, 2010), 5.

7. Timothy S. Lane, *Forgiving Others: Joining Wisdom and Love* (Greensboro: New Growth Press, 2004), 14–16.

Simple, Quick, Biblical

Advice on Complicated Counseling Issues
for Pastors, Counselors, and Individuals

MINIBOOK
CATEGORIES

- Personal Change
- Marriage & Parenting
- Medical & Psychiatric Issues

- Women's Issues
- Singles
- Military

USE YOURSELF | GIVE TO A FRIEND | DISPLAY IN YOUR CHURCH OR MINISTRY

New
Growth
Press

Go to **www.newgrowthpress.com** or call **336.378.7775** to
purchase individual minibooks or the entire collection.
Durable acrylic display stands are also available to house
the minibook collection.